SHADOW WORK GUIDED JOURNAL FOR MEN

RECLAIM YOUR WHOLENESS

By Dominica Applegate

Copyright © 2021

The information contained in this book is for general information purposes only and should not be considered a substitute for the advice of a mental health professional.

rediscoveringsacredness.com

FOR ALL WHO SUFFER

MOST OF THE SHADOWS
OF THIS LIFE ARE CAUSED
BY STANDING IN ONE'S
OWN SUNSHINE.

Ralph Waldo Emerson

TABLE OF CONTENTS

INTRODUCTION

Everyone has a dark side that holds known and unknown shadows. The parts we know about, we tend to repress or ignore due to feeling shame or fear. The parts we don't know about can haunt our inner and outer lives.

Shadow work is a time-tested tool that can help you face and integrate your shadow side. If you desire to experience more emotional and spiritual wholeness, consistent shadow work will be an important part of your journey.

You may wonder what could be hiding in your shadow side. What could you find as you shine the light of your consciousness into the dark? Common shadows include painful experiences, trauma, tough memories, negative thoughts, faulty belief patterns, secrets, fears, and more. There are also hidden talents and traits in the shadow.

Poet Robert Bly cleverly called the shadow, "A long bag that we drag behind us."

You feel it, don't you?

The heavy weight upon your shoulders?

Accumulated baggage?

Unhealed pain?

If you've never really taken an inner journey to do some exploration, then your shadow bag may be quite large and festering. The energy accumulated over the years doesn't just dissolve.

It grows in intensity and will come knocking on your door time and time again until you turn inward and face what's hidden. Perhaps it's time to begin an inner journey to deal with your deepest, darkest secrets, intense pain, shame, fears, regrets, or what some may call "demons."

Carl Jung, the brilliant mind behind the concept of the shadow, said it this way:

"Until you make the unconscious conscious, it will direct your life, and you will call it fate."

If you've got your hands on this shadow work journal, then it's likely you're ready to begin, or continue, your inner healing journey toward psychological wholeness.

Kudos for that.

The reality is that shadow work can be life changing. When done consciously and consistently, you can transform the dense energy of the shadow side into psychological and spiritual growth.

You can begin to fully own and embrace who you truly are – the light and the dark aspects of you – completely accepting your whole self.

What Is the Shadow?

According to Jung, the psyche, or mind, is comprised of various parts, including consciousness, ego identity, and the shadow, or unconsciousness. There's more to the concept, but let's keep it simple.

Essentially, from the time you are born, your mind takes the experiences, memories, traumas, negative emotions, and so on that the ego does not know how to process, or they're just too shocking, and exiles them into the shadow.

Into the unconscious. Out of sight, out of mind, right? So, your shadow side holds the fragmented parts of you that you cannot see or don't want to see. In other words, it holds a lot of pain and parts that we don't want to deal with.

The Shadow Side Is Not Bad or Evil

The shadow side is dark, but not because it's bad or evil. It's dark because it's yet to be illuminated by the light of your consciousness. You haven't gone within and flipped the light on just yet, or maybe you've only turned the dimmer lights on.

Shadow work is grabbing a floodlight and setting out on an inner journey to explore your unknown territories. It's casting light on the shadows that have been tripping you up or causing you pain.

Why would you want to go and rouse up painful shadows?

Because when you can illuminate, face, feel, and deal with those shadows, you release the pent-up energy associated with them.

You can integrate that accumulated energy back into your psyche, and as a result, experience more things like peace, joy, confidence, creativity, clarity, and contentment. You get to live from a space of feeling free, simply being who you are - all of you!

Here lies your hero's journey, a transformational inner journey toward greater self-discovery, meeting and embracing every aspect of you.

Here lies an opportunity to stop running, acknowledge the immense pain you feel, stop the self-loathing, let your walls fall, deal with what you've been hiding or self-medicating, and begin your inner healing journey. Compassionately own and embody your whole, awesome self, shadows and all.

If there's one thing I know, it's that we all desire to grow to become more peaceful, authentic, enlightened, compassionate, and loving. Shadow work is a valuable tool to help you fearlessly embrace your shadow side and awaken to your true, whole self.

Throughout history, there's been a lot of pressure put on men to act and be a certain way. You may feel pressured to be ultra-strong, ultra-confident, ultra-successful, ultra-independent, protect at all costs, keep your armor up, never fail, make big money, never cry, and so on.

It can feel quite overwhelming. It can also feel terrifying to reach out for help if you're struggling.

I am a firm advocate of seeking professional help from a qualified therapist, especially if one has experienced trauma. However, I know many men do not feel safe doing so, largely due to a lingering stigma around mental health counseling.

It is my desire that this journal may be a step in that direction, a path toward becoming curious about your inner world. Becoming interested in what's been exiled to your shadow bag for the purpose of facing, feeling, dealing, and integrating it.

Jung says, "There's no coming to consciousness without pain."

It's time to mine the shadow caves, seeking out what's wanting to be noticed and dealt with. Shadow work is not for the faint-hearted, but with courage and intent, you'll be well on your way to coming to know and love yourself on a whole new level.

How Will I Feel Doing Shadow Work?

Shadow work evokes different feelings or intensity of emotions for everyone. However, common emotions you may encounter along your journey are:

Fear

If you're like most men, the thought of going inside to face your deepest, darkest side elicits fear. My son recently told me that he has recurring nightmares where this huge, black blob is coming to devour him. He says he experiences sheer terror and wakes up abruptly. It's not uncommon for the shadow side to try to get our attention in dream time through frightening images.

This reminds me of something Jung said:

"The most terrifying thing is to accept oneself completely."

You may encounter fear as you answer some journal prompts. You may trigger some unhealed wounds or remember things that cause you to feel afraid. There may be experiences, trauma, or memories that you suppressed that aren't easy to face.

Remember that to heal it, you've got to face and <u>temporarily </u>feel it.

Anxiety

You may feel anxious at the thought of diving into your past. Again, the intensity will vary. I used to believe feelings of anxiety would literally kill me. I was wrong. I learned some anxiety-reduction breathing techniques and use them regularly. I also learned how to actually feel anxiety sensations in my body, and relax into them rather than resist, repress, or self-medicate.

If anxiety arises, take advantage of the many anxiety-reduction techniques available.

Shame

It's common to encounter feelings of shame or embarrassment. There may be plenty of shadows trying to keep you feeling disappointed and ashamed. Shadow work can help you silence and integrate such shadows, and this can feel quite freeing.

Anger

Some journal prompts may cause anger to surface, perhaps even rage. Even those who don't consciously feel angry may have shadows named anger or rage, especially if you're used to being a good boy because that's all that was acceptable in your home.

Shadow work can help you identify these emotions and learn how to express them in healthy, creative ways.

Numbness

You may feel emotionally numb as you try to answer some questions. Maybe you hardly ever feel emotion, or you're not sure how to handle the intensity, so you disconnect the mind from body. You may have numbed yourself with an addiction to alcohol, drugs, porn, sex, video games, or some other addictive behavior.

If you can't remember much about your childhood or past, you may have "shut down" your emotional GPS early on. Shadow work can help you begin to reconnect, remember, and deal and feel what wants to be healed in your shadow side.

Other emotions that may arise are guilt, regret, sadness, frustration, feeling abandoned, grief, and more.

If you start to feel like it's too much or too overwhelming, take some time to breathe slowly and deeply. Sit quietly or meditate for a bit and come back to journaling later. Take it at your own pace. There's no rush.

As you work through the prompts, consciously give yourself compassion and doses of love. Remember that as you work through the Shadow Work Journal, you're getting in there deep and re-collecting parts of you that you've chipped off over the years. You're becoming more whole.

Practicing Mindfulness & Meditation

No doubt diving into unknown inner territory can be tough. While it's great to illuminate your hidden talents and positive traits, discovering your deepest, darkest secrets, trauma, evil thoughts, twisted fantasies, mistakes, cruel behaviors, agonizing loneliness, and more can mess with the mind.

Adopting the practices of mindfulness and meditation can help.

What Is Mindfulness?

To be mindful means to consciously be in the present, aware of thoughts and feelings arising in the now. To be mindful is like being a thought detective. You're on the lookout for thoughts and emotions that arise. When you spot them, you flash them your badge.

Busted.

You do some investigating.

If the thoughts are negative or false, you get to say so. You get to call them out and say, "Excuse me. I see you, and I'm not falling for that. You're just blowing smoke again. I choose to believe and live in the truth and what you're saying just isn't true. Nothing you say can cause me to believe otherwise."

You also get to notice the positive thoughts or belief systems you've relegated to the shadow side.

"Oh, hey assertiveness. I see you. I'm sorry I banished you to the shadow. I welcome you back into my life, in balance, of course. I need you to help me deal with a boss that's totally taking advantage of my niceness."

To be more mindful means that you live more in the present, using your five senses to keep you grounded there. Throughout the day, take time to bask in the present. To see and hear what's around you, feeling the ground beneath your feet and noting any smells or tastes.

To learn more about mindfulness, check out the many excellent websites and articles online about the topic. You may even want to check into free mindfulness apps.

What Is Meditation?

Various forms of meditation can help one become more aware of "self" and gain better control of the thought life.

Meditation is taking time to get quiet with yourself. It's going within as a sacred act, allowing thoughts to come and go while remaining detached as a witness.

Thoughts are bound to arise, but we have the choice as to what types of thoughts we identify with and what types we ruminate on.

Not everyone wants to meditate, and that's alright. If that's you, then perhaps you can navigate your inner thoughts with a different practice or technique. However, if you'd like to become a regular meditator, do a bit of research to see what meditative techniques appeal to you.

As you commit to a regular meditation practice, you will experience plenty of benefits. Ultimately, you can get more acquainted with the "I" that is your core, spiritual nature. Your essence. The "I" underneath all those thoughts. The "I" outside of shadow and ego. You can connect with a space of peace and harmony within yourself as part of divine intelligence or whatever it is you call the power back of all things.

It's tempting to skip time to meditate. Taking time to just stop and be silent is challenging for many people. They're so accustomed to filling up every moment with something.

So, make that commitment, even if it's just five or ten minutes a day. Meditation is a discipline and a practice and can certainly help you as you navigate the shadow side of your ego.

Working Through Journal Prompts

Take your time working through the prompts. If you come across something too challenging, skip it. Maybe it's not time to "go there."

If you have experienced childhood or adult trauma, neglect, abuse, have been diagnosed with a mental health disorder, or you're simply not sure you want to confront your shadow side on your own, there are professional therapists that can help.

A counselor, spiritual advisor, wise friend, sponsor, etc., can oftentimes hold the space for you to begin processing and heal various wounds. There are Jungian or shadow work coaches, as well as trauma therapists, that cater to men.

Go easy on yourself. Remember that there's no right or wrong here. Cut yourself some slack as you delve deep into your psyche. You don't have to have it all figured out or have all the answers.

Do the work, but also allow your inner healing to unfold organically too. The psyche is a complex construct that oftentimes helps us integrate shadows naturally. In dream time, for example.

Finding and Loving the Real You

Your inner journey unearthing and integrating shadows not only helps you grow psychologically and emotionally but also spiritually. You're getting in there to expose your "false self" or your "ego identity". Why? So, you can awaken to the reality of your TRUE SELF or spirit. The you that you've forgotten about or lost over the years! That innocent, pure, lovable, compassionate, generous spirit.

My hope is that you experience deep and profound spiritual transformation, as well as compassion and divine Love for yourself and others as you discover and embrace your shadow side.

Remember, it's progress we're after, not perfection. Doing your inner healing work can be a sacred act. Give yourself permission to do it with grace and acceptance. Stay connected to your heart space as you move forward, focusing on your breath.

Shadow Work Tips:

You may get triggered by completing a question. A trigger is an intense feeling or reaction. Realize that this is an opportunity to begin facing, dealing, feeling, and healing. This means resisting the urge to project the uncomfortable emotions onto another. This means consciously working through them, feeling, and then releasing them, so they will lose their power or charge over you.

It's not "one and done."

Keep in mind that shadow work is not a one-size-fits-all approach to emotional, mental, or spiritual freedom. And it's also not a "one and done" kind of thing.

Shadows, or those memories, belief patterns, traits, stored energy, and so on, are often layered. You may face, feel, heal, and integrate one layer, or one fragment, only to have a variant or deeper version of it show up somehow down the road. I'm still contending with some deep, persistent shadows myself.

It's not enough to just learn about shadow work at the intellectual level. You want to learn and be able to apply it to your life consistently.

The following are four basic tips that can help you integrate shadows as you discover them via triggers, through journaling, through your nightly dreams, and so on.

1: NOTICE: ACKNOWLEDGE THE EMOTION OR FEELING THAT ARISES.

As a shadow hunter, from here on out, you're going to be on the lookout for what you're thinking and feeling at any given moment.

You're going to begin to notice when you feel emotionally triggered. As soon as you realize you're triggered, pause and acknowledge it.

Notice and feel the emotions momentarily. Recognize this is a trigger. The more intense the feelings, the bigger the shadow that's asking for your attention.

The sensations may feel intense at first, but know that by "feeling" it, you're working on "healing" and integrating it.

2: OBSERVE: OBSERVE SHADOWS AS A WITNESS.

You may discover plenty of things relegated to your shadow side, and not all of them are going to feel good.

However, remember that those emotions, thoughts, belief patterns, stories, traits, etc. are not arising to hurt you. They are part of your shadow side that the mind has been creating since you were born. And, you can witness them as more of a witness, which can decrease the intensity of feelings.

It helps to observe shadows as they arise from the perspective of your true self or spiritual nature. Refer to the thoughts or emotions that arise as "it," "you," "them," "exiled energy," etc.

For example, rather than saying, "I am depressed", you could say, "I see you, Depression. I feel you quite nicely right now." This way, you're not identifying solely as depression.

"I am unworthy" can be rephrased as, "I feel you, Unworthiness."

You can begin to witness shadows from the space of loving awareness, recognizing that the shadow part of you isn't reality. It's a created construct, just like your ego.

But it's not the real you as a spiritual being or consciousness.

3: QUESTION: DETAIN AND QUESTION IT

The next thing you can do is detain and question what's arising. Continue to act as a detective, doing some inner inquiry. You can ask things like, "Where did you come from?" "What do you want?" "Why do you keep popping up?" Feel free to journal the answers if you can at that moment.

4: INTEGRATE: CONSCIOUSLY INTEGRATE IT

Once you've felt it, acknowledged it, observed it, and questioned it, now it's time to lovingly bring it back into your psyche, otherwise known as integration.

Remember, emotions are energy in motion. They have messages for you. That repressed, suppressed, rejected energy wants to be seen, heard, and lovingly processed and released.

Rather than resist them, embrace and let the sensations move through you, dissolving into what may feel like more wholeness. Enjoy the peace that comes along with it.

Repeat these four steps each time you're contending with intense emotions that arise. Resist the urge to project your feelings onto others when you're emotionally agitated. Rather, do some inner inquiry before making a response.

It may only take a few moments, but it's worth it if it can help you heal and integrate shadows and save you from projecting your pain onto others.

This is a sacred time for you. You are shining the light of your consciousness into the darkness, not knowing what you'll find. That uncertainty can feel scary.

But take heart, this inner exploration can lead you to really understanding that you are not, nor have you ever been, that baggage that you've been lugging around.

Let the digging begin, as you walk your path toward rediscovering your beautiful sacredness.

"WHO LOOKS OUTSIDE, DREAMS; WHO LOOKS INSIDE, AWAKES." CARL JUNG

1   SHADOW HUNTING

The shadow side tends to hold plenty of negative thoughts. Take a few minutes to go *negative-thought shadow hunting*. Give your shadow side permission to speak to you all the negative thoughts swirling around in there. It may say things like: You're not worthy of happiness. You're such a screwup. No one likes you. You are so lazy.

Jot those thoughts down and take a good look at them. Then, confront your shadow-side. Tell it that those thoughts can't hurt you or keep you stuck any longer. Own your shadows, but also own the opposite. Say: "Yeah, maybe I am lazy at times, but I'm also quite energetic at times," or "Yes, at times I make mistakes, but I also get a lot of things right!"

As you shine the light of your consciousness on negative thoughts in the shadow side, you're witnessing them as parts of you that, at some point, you relegated to the shadow. They are part of you - not the real you, but the ego identity. Remember, you are, at your core, luminous energy - a spiritual creation - so try not to let negative thoughts keep you stuck in the mud any longer.

I AM WORTHY

MIRROR MIRROR

When is the last time you really looked at yourself in the mirror? I mean really gazed into your own eyes. Mirror work is a powerful tool for shadow work. I used to avoid eye contact at all costs because I thought everyone would only see my shadows. That's all I could see about myself at the time.

But what about beyond the shadow side? The deeper, more authentic, spiritual self? That's what you're looking for when you do mirror work. That's what you're aiming for; to more fully discover and embody.

Take time regularly to get in front of a mirror and gaze into your eyes. Take a minute or two and stare into YOU. Notice what thoughts or feelings arise. Does it feel weird? Scary? Silly? Can you see past your shadow side? See if you can sense yourself as luminous spirit.

I AM OPEN

3   ENVY

Do you envy what other people have? Their possessions? Success? Traits? Do you long for things in a way that makes you feel discontented?

What is it that you envy? Be specific.

Could this point to a shadow called low self-esteem or inferiority? Go within and see. Dialogue with what arises, with love and compassion.

_____

_____

_____

_____

_____

_____

_____

_____

_____

_____

_____

_____

_____

_____

_____

_____

_____

I AM ENOUGH

4 SHADOW INVITE

Draw a circle and imagine that it's your shadow side. Do you know some of the thoughts, beliefs, emotions, memories, or traits that might be in it? Write down what you're aware of and invite other shadows to surface. As you do this exercise, be aware of the reality that those things in your shadow side are parts of you relegated there over the years. Be gentle with them. Witness them with compassion and invite them to "integrate" back into your psyche. Balance it out.

Write about what you observe and feel while doing this exercise.

I HAVE A DARK SIDE, BUT
IT DOESN'T RULE ME.

SHADOW WORK

IS THE PATH
OF THE
HEART
WARRIOR.

Carl Jung

Since you've been hunting down shadows, you've probably aroused some shadows you weren't aware of before. Write a letter to your shadows to the negative shadows or those parts you aren't crazy about seeing. (Rage, fear, laziness, pride, lust, depression, etc.) Write from the perspective of your true, spiritual self. Your compassionate self.

Witness and acknowledge those negative shadows with love and compassion. Realize that although you may struggle with feeling _____ at times, you are NOT that particular shadow.

{*Hey rage. I feel you. At times, I feel like I AM you. However, I know the true me is pure bliss and peace. I know you have your reasons for camping out in the shadow, but I want you to know I see you and hear you. Let's figure out how to release and integrate you in healthy, creative ways.*}

_____

_____

_____

_____

_____

_____

_____

_____

_____

_____

_____

_____

_____

_____

I AM COURAGEOUS

MATURE MAN

Do you view yourself as mature? What does "being mature" mean to you?

Are there times when you act immaturely? If so, when?

If you were to ask your loved ones how mature they consider you, what do you think they'd say?

_____

_____

_____

_____

_____

_____

_____

_____

_____

_____

_____

_____

_____

_____

_____

_____

_____

_____

_____

_____

_____

_____

_____

STAY THE COURSE

SEXUALITY

Shining the light of consciousness on sexual shadows naturally occurs as you journey within. Do you feel shame, guilt, fear, disgust, or insufficiency around sex or sexuality?

If so, why? Don't judge yourself. Show compassion for yourself as you write about this topic.

RELATIONSHIP CHECK

Relationships tend to mirror or reflect to us some shadows - both positive and negative. How are your relationships in general? Any toxic relationships? If so, with who? Looking back, do you spot a pattern in your relationships? (Codependency, insecurity, jealousy, addiction, cruelty, etc.)

I AM GROWING

9   COMPASSION

What does being compassionate mean to you? Do you consider yourself to be compassionate toward others? If so, in what ways? Do you have compassion for yourself?

Explore the topic. If you tend to be compassionate toward others, yet heartless toward yourself, contemplate why this occurs. Check for self-loathing. And, as always, remember that no matter what, you are worthy of your own love and compassion.

I AM COMPASSIONATE

10 THAT'S ATTRACTIVE

Many times, when we enter a romantic relationship, we are attracted to things in the other that we lack. When you met your current or past partner, what did you see in them that you lacked? What attracted you to them? (Confidence, physical attributes, maturity, generosity, etc.)

At times, we're energetically attracted to another because we sense in that person things that we have lost or given away. Or, they could have strengths that we're lacking. Opposites do attract each other a lot. We can complement each other when it's operating at a secure and healthy level.

But we don't have to chase others based solely on traits that are underdeveloped in ourselves. Is it possible you did this? Tried to feel worthy based solely on their approval? Got with them just for emotional security or to not feel alone?

Explore the topic. Those things that you find attractive about others, can you go within and cultivate some of those things yourself? (Confidence, security, worthiness, unconditional love, etc.)

I AM RESILIENT

11   HO'OPONOPONO PRACTICE

The Ho'oponopono is a Hawaiian practice of self-forgiveness that can help you clear out negative thoughts toward yourself. There are four steps.

Take a slow, relaxing breath.
Say, "I'm sorry. Please forgive me. Thank you. I love you."

How do you feel saying this? Is it possible there are parts of you in your shadow that would benefit from hearing these words? A wounded inner child? An angry inner child? An abandoned inner child?

Go ahead and expand on this in writing. Think about the ways you've judged, sabotaged, or neglected yourself. Repeat the Ho'oponopono prayer often.

_____

_____

_____

_____

_____

_____

_____

_____

_____

_____

_____

_____

"Deep down, below the surface of the average man's conscience, he hears a voice whispering, "There is something not right," no matter how much his rightness is supported by public opinion or moral code." C. Jung

COMPETITION

Are you competitive? If so, how does that show up in your life? How do you feel about competition in general? What would unhealthy competition look like for you?

As a child, were you competitive? If so, what messages did you receive from your parents or other adults about it?

_____

_____

_____

_____

_____

_____

_____

_____

_____

_____

_____

_____

_____

_____

_____

_____

_____

_____

_____

_____

_____

I'M OWNING MY SHADOW SIDE

13   RUNNER?

When you experience conflict or contrast with someone, do you get out of there as fast as possible?

Are you a runner? Do you make it a habit to "ghost" others?

If so, do you know anyone else in your family who has similar behavior?

I AM COMMITTED

MASKING

You're likely familiar with wearing various "masks" to present yourself to the world in a certain way. What kinds of masks do you wear? How do you want others to see you?

Wearing a mask has its place, but keep in mind a mask can also hide your true nature. Your authentic nature.

Think about the kinds of things you don't want others to see or know about you. Maybe you wear an "I've got it all together" mask, but inside, you're feeling fear and burnout. Or perhaps you hide away an addiction or work hard to make it look like you're financially secure, but you're swimming in debt.

Get real with yourself. You can dig up some shadows that are simply longing to be faced, healed, and integrated. As you continue your shadow work journey, you'll wear less masks and be able to show up as your authentic self.

I AM ALIGNED

HIDDEN TRAITS

Make a list of three people you admire and/or love deeply.

What are the positive things you like about them?

Do you see any of those traits within you?

Is it possible some of those positive traits are hidden in your shadow-side longing to be seen and integrated?

_____

I BALANCE THE OPPOSITES

DISTRACTION

Do you get distracted easily? Mentally preoccupied? If so, how does distraction show up for you? Why do you think it's tough for you to stay in the present moment? What are you getting out of being distractable?

A man who is unconscious of himself acts in a blind, instinctive way and is in addition fooled by all the illusions that arise when he sees everything that he is not conscious of in himself coming to meet him from outside as projections upon his neighbour. Carl Jung

"When we find ourselves in a midlife depression, suddenly hate our spouse, our jobs, our lives, we can be sure that the unlived life is seeking our attention.

When we feel restless, bored, or empty despite an outer life filled with riches, the unlived life is asking for us to engage.

To not do this work will leave us depleted and despondent, with a nagging sense of ennui or failure. As you may have already discovered, doing or acquiring more does not quell your unease or dissatisfaction. Neither will "meditating on the light" or attempting to rise above the sufferings of earthly existence.

Only awareness of your shadow qualities can help you to find an appropriate place for your unredeemed darkness and thereby create a more satisfying experience. To not do this work is to remain trapped in the loneliness, anxiety, and dualistic limits of the ego instead of awakening to your higher calling."

Robert A Johnson

ADDICTIONS

Do you think you are addicted to something? If so, what is it? (Alcohol, drugs, food, sex, video games, work, porn, thinking, shopping, etc.)

Do you think addiction is a decoy so that you can't see what's going on in your shadow side? Numbing the inner pain?

Avoiding the past trauma, abuse, neglect, etc.?

I AM HONEST

THESE THOUGHTS!

What negative thoughts seem to plague your mind the most? If you sit quietly long enough, some will start to rise.

Write them down. Then, cross them out. These thoughts are not you. They are a byproduct of life experiences.

Where do you think you picked up these types of thoughts/beliefs?

_____

_____

_____

_____

_____

_____

_____

_____

_____

_____

_____

_____

_____

_____

_____

_____

_____

_____

_____

REST THE MIND

HOW DARE YOU?

Do you feel like you're being judged by others?

If so, what do you think they're judging you for?

Do you believe that these opinions are valid?

I TRUST MY HIGHER SELF

INSECURITY

Do you think you are insecure? On a scale of 1-10, how insecure do you think you are? Do you feel more insecure with certain people? If so, who? Does insecurity cause problems for you in relationships?

Do you feel insecure at certain times more than others? Explore the topic further. If you don't know your Attachment Style, feel free to do further research.

_____

_____

_____

_____

_____

_____

_____

_____

_____

_____

_____

_____

_____

_____

_____

_____

_____

_____

I ENJOY FEELING SAFE

FEARS

What are your biggest fears? Do you know why you are afraid of these things? Did something happen to cause this fear, or is it unknown? Have you ever talked to anyone about them?

Explore the topic. Take a deep breath and relax as you write. As you think about these things, notice how your body is feeling. Do you notice any sensations? Stay with them momentarily, allowing them to express and release. If this exercise feels overwhelming, skip it.

I CAN FACE FEAR

EXPECTATIONS

What do you feel those closest to you expect of you? What about society?

Do you have any intense feelings surrounding this?

Do you feel pressure? How do you handle it?

_____

_____

_____

_____

_____

_____

_____

_____

_____

_____

_____

_____

_____

_____

_____

_____

_____

_____

_____

Do you tend to respond or have a strong reaction when conflict arises? How about when someone comes to you with an issue? Do you overreact? If so, what seems to trigger you most?

Keep in mind that if you're triggered, it's you that has the explosives inside your shadow side. Blaming the person who hit your trigger button doesn't heal and integrate YOUR shadows. An intense reaction can indicate that your shadow side is active and wanting your attention. How do you feel about that?

PAUSE + BREATHE

VICTIM MENTALITY

Life can plow us over at times, leaving us feeling shattered and heartbroken. Painful circumstances and experiences may come, but we don't have to live life feeling like a victim.

Do you have a victim mentality? Always pointing your fingers at others and blaming them for your plight? If so, why do you feel that way?

Imagine you can fly and rise above all those things that have happened to you in life that have caused you to feel powerless. Do you believe you can go on about your life experiencing more peace, joy, and love? Can you take back your power?

EMPOWERED

Do you feel like you're supported by life? Or do you feel you have to do everything yourself? Do you feel alone? Who could you count on 100 percent if you needed something?

If you feel like you're on your own or are ultra-independent, reflect on how supported you felt growing up. Did you feel your primary caregivers had your back? If not, do you think perhaps you may have relegated some things to your shadow as a youngster?

Things like anger, fear, confusion, feeling abandoned, and unworthiness? If you tend to be ultra-independent, what do you think it would feel like to have a solid support system? Your tribe. In what ways could you work toward making this a reality.

Do you have any negative habits? If so, what are they?

Are they causing you some emotional mayhem? How about relationship struggles?

Can you recall when you first picked up the negative habits?

Explore the topic. What do you gain from each negative habit?

What shadows could be hiding underneath your bad habits?

WALK YOUR OWN JOURNEY.
BE UNIQUELY YOU.

Have you ever sabotaged yourself? Destroyed possibility for good things? Stayed stuck in limited belief patterns that didn't serve you? (I'm nothing but a screwup. I'll never amount to anything. I suck at relationships.)

Self-sabotage typically begins in childhood as a defense mechanism to help you adjust to a challenging situation or trauma. You may have tossed various parts of you into your shadow bag that are now asking to be faced, felt, healed, and brought back or integrated.

Explore the topic. Are you sabotaging long-term goals? If so, how? (Addiction, procrastination, perfectionism, self-criticism, etc.)

Be mindful of your thoughts and emotions. They'll let you know if you're unconsciously destroying the possibility of a rich, meaningful life.

THE ENNEAGRAM

How well do you know your traits, patterns, or personality? Take some time to take an Enneagram Personality Test over at The Enneagram Institute. Once you find your primary Type, do some investigating into the positive and negative traits associated with it.

Look at the most positive or healthiest traits. Which ones do you consistently embody?

Then, look at the traits considered unhealthy or negative. Do you identify with any of these? If so, do you believe you can come to overcome or integrate them? Do you believe you can reach the highest level of traits?

JUDGEMENTS

Do you judge others? If so, what do you find yourself judging consistently? Attitudes? Behaviors? Physical attributes?

Do a bit of exploring to see if any of the things you judge others for are within you. Do some digging and be honest. It's not uncommon to discover that the very things we point our fingers at in others are hiding in our shadow side. This could very well be an opportunity to integrate such shadows.

_____

_____

_____

_____

_____

_____

_____

_____

_____

_____

_____

_____

_____

_____

_____

_____

_____

I AM NON-JUDGMENTAL

Do you play small or big in life? Do you settle for crumbs? Minimize your potential? Shrink down? Or do you believe in your unlimited potential? In what ways do you play small or big?

If you do minimize your potential, why do you think that is? Where do you think this originated? Think about your family. Has anyone else played small?

How can you step into your power? Manifest the greatness within? Own your life in a way that helps you, but also helps the world?

For this exercise, think of someone recently who has hurt you terribly. As you reminisce, notice the emotions that arise, as well as the sensations occurring in your body. Do you tighten up? Does your heart rate increase? Do you feel heat or tingling?

Now, think about your past. Can you remember a time when you were young and felt similar? Who was it that caused you to feel this hurt? Write about the situation. As you do, focus on relaxing. Breathe slowly, deeply. If you begin to feel like you can't handle it, stop the exercise. Try it another time.

If you can, write down what you'd like to say to that person who hurt you when you were young. Be honest, knowing that that person cannot hurt you right now. Remind yourself that in this present moment, you are safe.

More writing space on next page

I AM HEALING

"OUR HEART GLOWS, AND SECRET UNREST
GNAWS AT THE ROOT OF OUR BEING.
DEALING WITH THE UNCONSCIOUS HAS
BECOME A QUESTION OF LIFE FOR US."
CARL JUNG

UNCONDITIONAL LOVE

Do you love others without conditions? Without expectations? No strings attached?

Unconditional love doesn't mean "anything goes." Healthy boundaries are important. However, loving without conditions means that you choose to love another despite their faults, quirks, mistakes, and so on. You choose to be a safe container that can hold them – all of them – without using control around love.

Do you think others feel safe enough to be themselves around you? Do you think they feel that you love them without conditions?

How do you feel about crying? Do you feel free to cry if you want or need? Or do you feel like crying is a sign of weakness? That you'll be judged? If so, where did you get that message? How would you feel if you felt 100% free to release the tears occasionally?

Some shadow parts that have been banished to the shadow side may very well be tears longing to be released.

_____

_____

_____

_____

_____

_____

_____

_____

_____

_____

_____

_____

_____

_____

_____

_____

_____

_____

FREE TO RELEASE

EMOTIONAL DISCONNECT

Do you feel emotionally numb? Do you feel separate from your emotions? Emotionally detached? Have others told you that you're emotionally distant? Do you find it challenging to connect with others at an emotional level?

Explore the topic. If you experienced trauma (abuse, neglect, etc.) as a child, you might have cut off your emotions as a defense mechanism.

"Shut down mode" is a survival mechanism that served you then but may not be serving you well as an adult. If this resonates, you may want to explore the topic further with a qualified trauma or somatic experiencing therapist.

FREE TO FEEL

What are your major complaints about others? Things that really get on your nerves. Think about your family, friends, coworkers, and people in general. Make a list of your top complaints.

Then, go within and ask those shadows that are most triggered about these things to step forward. See what arises and have an inner dialogue with them.

For example, let's say you get super annoyed when someone becomes emotional. Why do you think that is? What shadow part of you gets "triggered" when you encounter emotions? Fear? Anger? Selfishness?

_____

_____

_____

_____

_____

_____

_____

_____

_____

_____

_____

_____

_____

_____

_____

_____

MEMORY DELETION

Memories are snapshots of the past. While we are grateful that the mind can store memories, there may be some memories that we'd rather not remember. They may evoke negative feelings like shame, guilt, regret, fear, anger, and so on.

Think about a memory that tends to elicit negative emotions within you, but rather than letting the emotions overtake you, close your eyes and notice where you feel these emotions or sensations in your body.

Do you feel them in your gut? Your chest area? Can you describe the sensations? Breathe through them. Let them run their course.

Now, what if you could delete the emotional charge from this memory? Just tap that button and, poof: gone. As you consciously face and feel the charged energy from memories (shadow parts), you invite them to heal and integrate. Write about your experience.

Do others tend to demean or belittle you? Did you experience this while growing up?

If so, explore how this made you feel. How did (do) you cope with these feelings? Do you shut down or disconnect? Repress the emotions? Fight back?

Do people tend to demean you over and over? If so, what can you do to learn better boundary-setting skills?

_____

_____

_____

_____

_____

_____

_____

_____

_____

_____

_____

_____

_____

_____

_____

_____

_____

_____

_____

ENERGY VAMPIRES

Are there people in your life that tend to drain you? They pull at you emotionally and/or physically? Why do you think this is happening? Are you able to address the situation in a healthy way? Have a conversation? Set boundaries? Is this a pattern that's been going on throughout your life? Does going into "fix it" mode help you feel worthy, even though you feel drained?

I AM INFINITE LOVE

You have feelings, but do you feel like you ARE your feelings?

Are you observing them or being them?

(I feel angry vs. I am anger) (I feel sad vs. I am sadness.)

Part of shadow work is coming to understand that your true Self is not thoughts or emotions. Not the ego or the shadows; they are constructs that help you navigate life here on planet Earth. Rather, your true Self is something far greater – a conscious spirit. The observer.

Look at Carl Jung's model of the psyche. Write about your thoughts on the conscious and the unconscious parts of you.

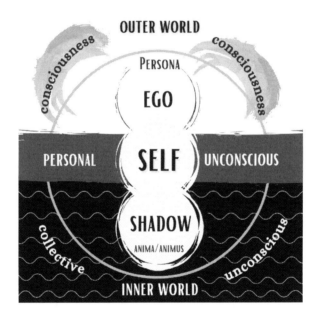

"I AM NOT WHAT HAPPENED TO ME,
I AM WHAT I CHOOSE TO BECOME."

CARL JUNG

One does
not become
enlightened
by imagining
figures of light,
but by making
the darkness
conscious.

Carl Jung

REPRESSION

What emotions do you tend to repress regularly? What don't you want to feel? Anger? Rage? Fear? Shame? Guilt? It's easy to think such emotions are "wrong", but emotions aren't necessarily right or wrong. Emotions are energy, and they have messages for you. Consider them your inner navigation system.

If you can identify intense emotions you tend to repress regularly, such as rage, begin dialoguing with these parts of you without judgment. Feeling rage isn't a "bad" thing. It's learning how to face, feel, and express it in creative ways that cause no harm to you or others. In other words, expressing it in healthy ways.

Bottling up or suppressing intense emotions creates a denser, heavier shadow bag. Breathe. Lean into the emotions and learn creative ways to let them express themselves. Exercise it out. Dance it out. Write it out. Punch it out using pillows or a punching bag. Talk it out. All in balance, of course. Make a game plan for you for the times intense emotions start to rise within. Then, practice.

I FULLY ACCEPT MYSELF

It's easy to feel like a partner will make you feel whole. Listen to love songs, and many are about just that: finding a person who will complete you. The reality, however, is that one person cannot make you feel complete or "whole."

Have you gone into a relationship thinking that person will complete you? If so, can you see where you gave some of your power away in thinking this way? What are some things you can start doing to feel more "whole" single and in a relationship?

How can you nurture your mind, body, and spirit? Are you investing some time daily sitting quietly and going within? Are you doing some "inner healing work"?

"WHERE LOVE RULES, THERE IS NO WILL TO POWER, AND WHERE POWER PREDOMINATES, LOVE IS LACKING. THE ONE IS THE SHADOW OF THE OTHER." CARL JUNG

VALUES

What are your major values? What do you feel are the most important things in life? Here are some common values: Courage, honesty, integrity, confidence, humility, kindness, authenticity, faith, trust, freedom, health, family, respect, community, spirituality, love, and responsibility.

How often do you consciously think about your most cherished values? What happens when others don't honor your values? How do you respond or react?

_____

_____

_____

_____

_____

_____

_____

_____

_____

_____

_____

_____

_____

_____

_____

_____

_____

I VALUE LIFE

SELF-CARE

On a scale of 1-10, how well do you practice self-care? Things like getting enough sleep, eating nutritious foods, taking time for yourself, maintaining healthy boundaries with others, resting, and feeding yourself positive things mentally, emotionally, and spiritually.

Do you tend to over-give to others and then complain about burnout? If so, what could this mean in terms of priorities? How can you practice taking better care of yourself? Make a plan.

_____

_____

_____

_____

_____

_____

_____

_____

_____

_____

_____

_____

_____

_____

_____

_____

_____

_____

_____

I CARE FOR MYSELF

LITTLE ME

Sometimes people refer to shadows as the wounded "inner child" or "inner children." Think of it like this. When you experience overwhelming or traumatic things as a youngster, you're too young to "process" those emotions. The ego just isn't strong enough when we're little. So, it relegates those experiences, memories, beliefs, situations, emotions, etc. to the shadow side.

This may have served you back then, but now, as an adult, those exiled parts will make themselves known to be processed and integrated.

Find a picture of you when you were little. Consider framing it and putting it on your nightstand, on your altar if you have one, or somewhere in your home where you'll see it often. Use this picture as a reminder that there may be parts of you that want/need attention in your shadow side from time to time. You can also let it remind you of the innocent, worthy spirit that you truly are.

BE SILENT + LISTEN

SHADOW MONSTER

Here's a visualization exercise to help you choose to love yourself - your whole self - without conditions. Close your eyes. Picture yourself walking through tunnels in a dark cave, using a flashlight to make your way. You turn a corner, and your light falls on someone curled up in a fetal position in the corner. They cower in fear, not wanting to be seen.

As you move closer, you notice that this person is you. It's your shadow side covered in mud. There are spiders and snakes all over. As you move closer, you notice how petrified your shadow side is, ashamed that it'll be seen as filthy and useless.

Approach your shadow side with gentleness, compassion, and love. Let the light of your lantern reveal the truth: that your shadow side is clean. That the cave is but an illusion, and you are both surrounded by white light. Go and sit beside your shadow side and put your arm around them. Comfort them. Begin a loving dialogue, letting them know that they don't have to stay hiding in the darkness. That it's safe to come out and enjoy life.

Note how you felt doing this exercise. How did you feel as you saw your shadow side cower in fear? How can this be a turning point for your life?

ENJOY THE JOURNEY

In what ways do you avoid pain?

How do you avoid being hurt?

Dig deep and get very honest with yourself. Are these attitudes or behaviors truly helping you or not?

Explore the topic.

_____

_____

_____

_____

_____

_____

_____

_____

_____

_____

_____

_____

_____

_____

_____

_____

_____

_____

Do you consider yourself open-hearted or closed off?

Has anyone ever told you that you're shut down? Cold as ice? Emotionally detached?

If so, are you willing to explore this topic? Delve inside to see if there are some shadows or old wounds/trauma wanting to be faced, seen, and processed?

_____

_____

_____

_____

_____

_____

_____

_____

_____

_____

_____

_____

_____

_____

_____

_____

_____

_____

_____

_____

I CHOOSE OPENNESS

Who are those you admire most? Your heroes?

What is it about them that you dig so much?

List the traits you love about them.

Now, go within and see if you recognize those traits within you. If they're not obvious, do you think they could be hiding in your shadow side, also known as the "golden shadows"?

_____

_____

_____

_____

_____

_____

_____

_____

_____

_____

_____

_____

_____

_____

_____

_____

_____

_____

OWN YOUR TALENTS

Do you spend most of your time thinking about yourself, others, or the whole world? One hierarchy of worldviews explores four developmental stages. You can learn a lot about yourself by seeing what stage you're tied to most. Explore the stages and see where you identify.

Egocentric (I am most important.)
Ethnocentric (My family/religion/tribe is most important.)
Worldcentric (All humans matter regardless of race, religion, etc.)
Kosmocentric (I value and support all humans, the planet, and the cosmos.)

take a walk
on the wild side

NEGATIVITY

Think about two or three negative traits you've been identifying with. Now, get in front of a mirror and own both sides of that trait.

For example, if you circled "selfish," look at yourself and say, "I am selfish!" Repeat it over and over with conviction until it loses its charge over you. As you identify with a shadow part, you're stripping it of its power over you. You're decreasing resistance, which allows those negative emotions to come and go like the wind, rather than stay stuck in the shadow part of you and unconsciously drive your life.

Remember that on the opposite side of each negative trait, there's a positive. (Anger/happiness, fear/faith, selfishness/generosity.) When you can integrate the repressed part that typically comes out as a strong reaction, you'll experience more of the positive aspects!

Write about this experience.

_____

_____

_____

_____

_____

_____

_____

_____

_____

_____

_____

_____

_____

_____

BALANCE THE OPPOSITES

MASCULINITY

On a scale of 1-100, how masculine do you feel you are? How feminine?

Are you comfortable with this? If someone called you feminine, what would you feel? How would you respond?

DEAR SELF

Life doesn't always go as planned. It's likely you've made some choices that you now regret. There may be shadows in your shadow bag as a direct result of poor choices and/or decisions.

Today, write a letter to your shadow side.

Be understanding and show compassion. Be gentle and forgiving. You can look back on this letter in the future for the times you need some encouragement.

Your shadow side may seem completely dark, but you may find some gold when you get in there and start digging around. Not all repressed or hidden aspects of yourself are "negative". It's likely you've disconnected or tossed positive traits into your shadow bag too, such as artistic talent, assertiveness, intuition, creativity, and more.

Do some digging. Remember what you used to love as a child. What were you passionate about? What have you put on the shelf?

Retrieve the golden shadow.

MINE FOR YOUR GOLD

Is there anyone in your life with who you feel safe enough to share your deepest, darkest thoughts or feelings? Your struggles? Fears? Strong emotions? Primal anger? Those darkest thoughts, strong impulses, and primal emotions, others have experienced the same things. You're not as alone as you may feel.

Denying or continually repressing your darkest side can grow a huge shadow bag that can wreak havoc on your emotions and behaviors. At some point in life, it's helpful to find someone who can hold a safe space for you to share whatever it is you're ashamed or afraid to share. You can also get it out in writing — those thoughts, fears, intense emotions, primal urges, rage — they are not the real "you," and they can be integrated into your whole psyche, ultimately helping you feel more whole.

TRUST THE PROCESS

When was the last time you felt super angry? What caused you to feel this anger?

How did you handle the intense emotions? How do you usually contend with anger?

Become curious and do some exploration around anger and common triggers.

BELIEFS

Do you have beliefs that you don't want anyone bucking? If so, what are they? Why do you think you are so protective of these beliefs?

Does this arouse fear? Can you imagine letting others disagree with your beliefs without getting charged up about it?

EMBRACE REALITY

ROLLER COASTER

Visualize your whole self, shadows and all, standing in line to get on a roller coaster. From the perspective of a wise sage, what would you say to yourself to prepare for the ride?

The incline? The decline? The loops? The emotions that might arise?

Correlate this with life. Write a letter to yourself about your future and the roller coaster you're likely to ride. What can you say to ease tension, negative feelings, or get excited about the thrill of it all?

_____

_____

_____

_____

_____

_____

_____

_____

_____

_____

_____

_____

_____

_____

_____

_____

"WE MEET OURSELVES TIME AND AGAIN IN A THOUSAND DISGUISES ON THE PATH OF LIFE." CARL JUNG

UNDERLYING STORIES

Think about your primary caregivers. Can you think of an underlying story that might have been running their lives? Hidden beliefs? These can be positive or negative.

Just start writing what comes to mind about Mom or Dad. For example, if Dad was addicted to alcohol, what kind of story do you think was running in his mind?

"I can't do this. Life is hard. It's too hard to face these feelings. Life sucks. I suck. I'm a failure. I'm scared. Nothing ever goes my way. I'm worthless," and more.

If Dad was happy and successful, it might have been totally different. He might have thought: "I'm worthy. I'm diligent. I believe life is for me. I work hard. Things go my way."

Take some time writing about Mom and Dad. Then, go through and see if you identify with some of the underlying thoughts or stories. What are they? Look for the negatives and know that those are some of the shadows that may have been passed onto you. Acknowledge them and keep doing your own inner healing work to integrate them.

More writing space on next page

AIM FOR WHOLENESS

CAGED RAGE

Do you have caged rage? If so, how do you feel about this? Do you feel shame, fear, or alone?

Do you believe you could find constructive, creative ways to release pent-up anger or rage?

Explore the topic, as there are healthy ways to own and release the shadow of rage.

SELF-AWARENESS

You're becoming more self-aware, integrating your shadow-side into your whole psyche.

How does this make you feel? As you near the completion of this journal, take note of the journey.

What tripped you up the most? Why do you think that is?

_____

_____

_____

_____

_____

_____

_____

_____

_____

_____

_____

_____

_____

_____

_____

_____

_____

_____

_____

_____

CREATIVE VISION

Write a short story in the present tense of the kind of life you truly desire. Be as specific as you desire — there's no right or wrong here.

What's happening? What's important to you? How are you feeling?

For example, *"Life is so amazing right now. I feel freer and more at peace than I've ever felt before. I wake up grateful most days. My career is going well. I'm loving my relationship. We are connected at the heart level and growing individually and together. When challenges come, I'm not drowning in fight, flight, or shut down mode. I'm living mindful, expecting goodness, and committed to showing up as my authentic self. Life is a roller coaster and I'm learning doing my best to enjoy the ride!"*

CONGRATULATIONS!

Robert A Johnson wrote, "To own one's own shadow is to reach a holy place - an inner center - not attainable in any other way."

Your story is important, all of it. As you worked through the prompts, I hope you were able to come to know your whole self much better.

I also hope that you have been able to own and integrate parts of your shadow that have been tripping you up in some fashion. And that you've gained a lot of insight and discovered a lot of treasures too.

Be proud of yourself for showing up and doing the work. Make a solid commitment to continue with this type of whole-making journey.

There are likely to be more layers, triggers that show up out of nowhere, and some surprises as you navigate life's road. Life tends to offer plenty of props or mirrors so that we can continually be learning, healing, growing, and evolving.

But it can all lead to greater experiences of peace and joy.

If you find yourself struggling now or in the future, consider reaching out to a professional therapist. It's worth the investment.

Stay present. Mindful. Breathe. Stay true to you.

Offer gratitude for it all.

Dominica

About the Author

Dominica Applegate is an author who is passionate about helping others heal, grow, and evolve. She's especially interested in using her experiences and her story to encourage others.

For over twelve years, she's reached many people globally with inspirational writings about waking up, doing inner healing work, creating healthier relationships and enjoying a more meaningful life.

Professionally, she's equipped with a graduate degree in counseling and over ten years' experience working in the mental health field. Personally, she's been a serious seeker since her late teens, immersing herself in various spiritual practices.

Her books include:

- Healing After a Breakup: A 50-Day Devotional & Guided INNER WORK Journal

- Into the Wild Shadow Work Journal: Reclaim Your Wholeness

- Goodbye Codependency: A 40-Day Devotional & Guided Journal to Boost Self-Care

- The Pain, It Shapes Her World {Poetry}

Learn more at rediscoveringsacredness.com

Made in United States
Troutdale, OR
12/16/2024

26730813R00049